Norse Mythology
A Guide To Ancient Viking Religion and Beliefs

DUSTIN YARC

DEDICATION

To polytheists, pagans, and religious reconstructionists everywhere.

CONTENTS

INTRODUCTION

Thank you for purchasing this copy of Norse Mythology.

The following chapters will discuss many aspects of Norse mythology and the overall beliefs of the Vikings.

You will discover the two main clans of Gods and Goddesses: the Aesir and Vanir, as well as answers to questions such as:

- How did the Norse people view the cosmos?
- Who was their version of Adam and Eve in their own mythology?
- What are the runes, and what is their origin story?
- What did the Norse believe happened to a person after they died?
- As well as many other amazing thing from Norse history and mythology.

There are plenty of books on this subject on the market, thanks again for choosing this one! Every effort was made to ensure it is full of as much useful information as possible. Please enjoy!

1 THE AESIR GODS AND GODDESSES

THE AESIR ARE one of two main clans of the Gods of the Norse pantheon. Aesir, pronounced ICE-ear, is the plural form of the word áss, which means "God." The Gods and Goddesses of the Aesir include many figures that are found in Scandinavian tales, including Tyr, Baldr, Thor, Frigg, and Odin. These Gods live in the realm of Asgard, which is separated from the mortal world of Midgard. The two places are connected by a rainbow bridge known as Bifrost. Asgard is one of the Nine Worlds and is found in the sunniest and highest branches of the world-tree Yggdrasil.

The Aesir belong to a very sophisticated group of cosmological, mythological, and religious belief systems. These views were shared by the Germanic and Scandinavian people. These traditions were first developed when significant culture and religions started to manifest, around 1000 BCE, until Christianity came to the area, which happened between 900 and 1200 CE.

Even though the beings that resided in Aesir were immortal, they were still thought to be more perishable than typical Indo-European immortals. The Aesir maintained their youth artificially from the golden apples of Ioun, and they could be killed as well.

The gods and goddesses of the Vanir and Aesir were viewed as contemporary figures that existed alongside each other, unlike in other polytheistic cultures where their Gods were seen as younger or elder compared to one another. These two main clans, the Vanir and Aesir, fought, exchanged hostages, and held treaties with each other. It is speculated that the difference between the Vanir and Aesir are reflective of the interactions that occurred between the different social classes of society during that time.

Odin

Odin is one of the main, and most complex, characters of Norse mythology. He is the head of the Aesir clan and had a tendency to venture from Asgard on solitary wanderings on self-interested quests. Odin was always looking to discover new things and loved sharing his wisdom. On the other hand, he had little regard for fairness, justice, common values, or for the respect of convention and law. He is the patron of outcasts and rulers, among other things.

Odin is also a war and poetry god and has qualities that are considered effeminate; conditions that would have brought shame to many ancient warriors. People that are looking for nobility, honor, and prestige would often worship him. He was also known to be a fickle trickster. Odin had quite an odd combination of characteristics, so how could one person house all of the qualities?

Odin can be translated to "Master of Ecstasy." When broken down into two parts, odr means "inspiration, fury, ecstasy," and –inn is a masculine definite article which means "the master of." The ecstasy that Odin has is what brings together the many different areas that he is associated with: the dead, poetry, shamanism, magic, wisdom, sovereignty, and war.

In pop-culture depictions of him today, he is viewed as the battlefield commander and honorable ruler, but he was nothing like that to the Norse. In comparison to the truly noble gods of war like Thor or Tyr, Odin would incite peaceful people to meaningless strife with sinister glee.

Odin didn't like to worry himself with the average warrior, and he preferred to lavish his blessings on the ones that he specifically considered worthy of his attention. He kept close affiliation with other warrior-shamans whose fighting and spiritual practices were centered on creating an ecstatic unification with totem animals, typically bears or wolves, and then through extension, to Odin himself. This means that as a war-god, he wasn't concerned with the reasons as to why there was a conflict, or what the outcome would be, but instead, he simply loved the chaotic and raw frenzy of battle itself.

The main difference between monotheistic and polytheistic theologies is that, with the former, God is viewed as all-knowing, powerful, and loving. Polytheistic gods are limited, just like the people they watch over. Odin considered all types of limitations as something he had to overcome, thus causing his quests to be carried out in a cruel manner to grow his wisdom, knowledge, and power.

One of Odin's common characteristics is his single eye. The story goes that Odin sacrificed his other eye in order to gain great wisdom. One day, he ventured out to Mimir's Well. Mimir, a shadowy figure, lived there and his knowledge was considered unparalleled. Mimir achieved most of his knowledge by drinking the magical water from the well, so Odin had come to ask Mimir for some of the water. Mimir refused to share the water unless Odin was willing to sacrifice his eye. Odin, either after deliberation or straight away depending on the particular rendition of the story, gouged out an eye and then dropped the eye into the well. Mimir then dipped his horn in the well and gave Odin a drink.

On a separate occasion, Odin set out to discover the runes, which are symbols carved on the trunk of Yggdrasil by the Norns. This book will discuss more about the runes, the mythical tree Yggdrasil, and the Norns later on. Odin watched the Norns as they carved thes symbols into the tree, and envied them for their wisdom and powers. The runes reside in the Well of Urd, and they only show themselves to people who prove they are worthy, Odin decided to hang himself from Yggdrasil, stabbed himself with a spear, and looked down into the waters of the well below. He wouldn't allow any of the other gods to help him in any way, not even with offerings of water. Odin stayed in this position for nine days and nights. On the ninth night, he began to see shapes in the well: the runes.

Thor

Thor is the most popular and prominent figure in Norse mythology. He is the archetype of an honorable and loyal warrior. Thor is the type of hero that all the human warriors aspired to be. He defended the Aesir fortress from the Giants, who are typically the god's enemies. His physical strength is unmatched, and his sense of duty and courage cannot not be shaken.

Thor wears a belt of strength that has remained unnamed, unlike his hammer. This belt doubles his formidability when worn. The most famous thing Thor owns is his hammer, Mjollnir, which means "lightning" in Old Norse. It's very rare for him to be seen without it. Thor was the embodiment of thunder, and his hammer was lightning. He would ride through the sky in his goat-drawn chariot slaying giants.

One of his biggest nemeses is the enormous sea serpent Jornungand, which encircles the human world of Midgard. In one legend where Thor was on a fishing trip, he tried to fish Jormungand from the ocean, and the only thing that stopped him was when his companion cut the line. Thor's battle with Jornungand ends when they kill each other during the great battle of Ragnarok.

It's ironic that Thor consistently protected his world from the Giants considering he was a three-quarters giant himself. Odin, his father, was a half-giant. Jord, his mother, was a full giant. This sort of lineage was standard among the gods and shows that the relationship that the giants and the gods had couldn't be completely described as hostile.

Thor played a big part in the fertility and agriculture of humanity. This is an additional extension of his abilities as a sky god, including that he made it rain so that the human's crops could grow. His wife, Sif, is also noted for having golden hair, which is assumed to be a symbol for fields full of grain. This made their marriage referred to as a hierogamy, which means divine marriage.

Mjolnir, the hammer of Thor, was depicted as a fearsome weapon which was able to level a mountain. Mjolnir was created by Brokkr and Sindri, dwarf brothers, and its short handle was caused by a mishap while they were building it. Legend tells it that Loki bet one of the dwarf brothers that they couldn't make an item that was more beautiful than items made from the Sons of Ivaldi. The rendition of the tale goes something as follows:

First Sindri places a pigskin into the forge and has his brother work the bellows until he tells him to stop. In the form of a fly, Loki bites Brokkr on his arm, but the dwarf doesn't stop working the bellows. Sindri then adds golden bristles from Freyr's boar into the forge and tells Brooke the same thing. Loki comes back again, and this time bites him on the neck twice. Brokkr works through the pain. Sindri removes Odin's ring Draupnir from the forge, which was created from the golden bristles, and then puts iron in and gives Brokkr the same order. Loki comes back again bites Brokkr harder, and on the eyelid this time, drawing blood in the process. When the blood drops into his eye, he has to stop working the bellows so he can wipe away the blood. Sindri then returns and removes Mjolnir. The handle ends up being shorter than it was supposed to be, causing it to have to be wielded with only one hand.

Even though it is flawed, they still win the bet and set out to get Loki's head. Loki manages to wiggle his way out of the bet though, by telling them that they will have to cut his neck to get his head, but his neck was never part of the gamble. As a consolation, Brokkr instead sews Loki's mouth closed.

Loki

Loki is known as the trickster god within Norse mythology. Even though Loki wasn't a god of a particular aspect of life such as love or war, he still had an equivocal and distinct role among the giants, gods, and other spiritual beings, and is mentioned in several myths.

Farbauti, a giant, is Loki's father. Laufey or Nal is his mother. It is unsure what exactly she was, a giantess, goddess, or something else. Loki fathered Hel, the underworld goddess, Jormungand, the serpent, and Fenrir, a wolf. Their mother was Angrboda, a giantess. This group is hardly reputable. As you will come to see, he didn't care about the well-being of the other gods. He also had another son, Narfi or Nari, with his wife, Sigyn.

Not only is he seen as running afoul of societal expectations, but he also crosses the lines when it comes to the laws of nature. Besides the children that he fathers (listed above,) he is also the mother of Sleipnir, which is Odin's horse. He gave birth to the horse after he turned himself into a mare and courted Svadilfari.

Loki is always seen as a cunning coward that is only interested in self-preservation and pleasures. He is typically somewhat helpful, yet malicious and playful. He is also disrespectful and extremely skeptical.

Unlike the other gods, Loki's name hasn't been able to be completely translated. Most have said that his name is unknowable, but the scholar Eldar Heid may have come across with a solution. He noticed that the name Loki showed up in contexts that compared him to a knot. In Icelandic, Loki became known as tangle or knot. With this knowledge, Loki could mean "Tangle" or "Knot."

The Tale of Loki's Binding

Loki was always more of a burden to the gods and goddesses than he was helpful. But after he caused the death of the beloved god Baldur and made sure that Baldur would stay in the underworld until the end of the universe, he started to go about and talk ill of the gods. Finally, the gods decided that his abuse had gone too far, and they set out to capture him.

Loki ran way from Asgard to the peak of a mountain. He even built himself a house that had four doors so that he was able to watch for pursuers from every direction. During the day he would transform into a salmon and hide in a waterfall nearby. At night he would sit next to a fire, weaving a net so that he could fish for food.

Odin was able to see where Loki was now dwelling, and the gods set out for him. When Loki spied his former friends approaching his home, he tossed the net into the flames and transformed into a salmon and hid in the stream. When the gods saw that he had thrown his net into the fire, they figured that he had switched himself into the image of the same things that he had intended to catch. The gods took some of Loki's twine that he had been using and started to build their own net. They then made their way over to the stream. They cast their net into the stream several times, and each time they barely missed the salmon. Finally, the salmon made a bold leap downstream to try and head for the sea. As he was in the air, Thor was able to catch him. The salmon started to wiggle in his grasp, but Thor held the fish by its tail fins. This is why salmon now have a thin tail.

Loki, in his regular form, was then taken to a cave. The gods then added two of Loki's sons, one of which they transformed into a wolf. The wolf quickly killed his brother and spread his insides across the floor of the cave. They then tied Loki to three rocks within the cave using the entrails of his son as the chains. Skadi laid a venomous snake on a rock that was positioned above his head so that its venom would drip onto Loki. Loki's wife came and sat with him and held a bowl under the snake to catch the venom. Now and then she had to empty the bowl, and that's when the poison would drip onto Loki and burn his skin. This caused him to shake violently, causing earthquakes to rip through Midgard. This was how Sigyn and Loki lived until Loki broke free and fought with the Giants in Ragnarok.

Frigg

Frigg, meaning beloved, is sometimes referred to as Frigga. She is the highest-ranking Aesir goddess. Frigg's husband is Odin, and she is Baldur's mother. When taking her ranking among the goddesses into consideration, there is little information about her attributes, deeds, and personality. Most of what is known about her aren't unique. She also shares many of her attributes with the goddess Freya. With similarity between the two, and their evolution from an earlier goddess, Fria, it's easy to see that they are often confused, especially in modern day.

Frigg was a seidr, a Norse magic practitioner. The seidr were concerned with figuring out what destiny was and re-weaving its course. She was also known as a sorceress. These types of people would travel from town and perform their acts of seidr for compensation such as food and lodging. Much like other shamans, her social status was vague. She was simultaneously despised, revered, atoned, longed for, feared, and praised, depending on who you asked.

Frigg was accused of infidelity. It is said that she slept with a slave. She also had relations with Vili and Ve, Odin's brothers, who were left in charge while Odin was exiled from Asgard.

Baldur

Baldur was the son of Frigg and Odin and was also the husband of Nanna, and father of Forseti. He was deeply loved by all the other gods and goddesses, as well as the humans. He was so merry, compassionate, and dapper that he gave off a glowing light.

One day, Baldur began to have dreams about his death. Frigg, his mother, started to travel the world and received a promise from every being and object that they wouldn't harm Baldur. The other gods were so confident in his invincibility that they began throwing things and weapons at him, and watches as they bounced off and left him unscathed.

Loki sensed a chance for some mischief. He asked Frigg if she had possibly overlooked anything during her quest for the oaths. She commented that she felt that the mistletoe was too harmless and small to worry about. Loki then made a spear from some mistletoe and talked the blind god Hodr into throwing the spear at Baldur. The spear pierced Baldur and killed him.

The gods then sent Hermod to the underworld to find out if they could keep Baldur out of the clutches of Hel. When Hermod arrived in the underworld, he found Baldur sitting next to Hel in a seat of honor. Hermod pleaded with Hel to release Baldur. Hel said she would if Hermod could get everything in the world to weep for him. He had to prove that Baldur was as beloved as Hermod made him out to be.

Everybody, except for Pokk, a giantess who is assumed to be Loki in disguise, wept for Baldur. Since Pokk didn't weep, Baldur stayed in his grave until Ragnarok. He then returned to the living, which gladdened the hearts of everybody.

DUSTIN YARC

2 THE VANIR GODS AND GODDESSES

THE VANIR, PRONOUNCED VAN-ear, are the second clan of Norse deities. Vanir likely comes from the root word wen, which means desire or pleasure. The most common members are Freyja, Freyr, and Njord.

The Vanir clan represented wealth, fertility, and exploration. According to one belief, the Vanir could be older that the Aesir, which may mean that the war between the Vanir and Aesir is an allegory for half-remembered religious and societal problems of the Norse culture from that time.

The Vanir live in Vanaheim, one of the Nine Worlds. One historian states that the Vanir may have once been a human tribe. They are associated more with magic than the Aesir. They also took part in endogamy and incest, meaning they would marry outside of their social class and within their family, both things that Norse culture at the time strongly frowned upon.

Freya

Freya, meaning lady, is one of the most distinguished goddesses of the Vanir tribe. She became an honorary goddess of the Aesir after the war. Njord is her father, but her mother is unknown. Some believe her mother to be Nerthus. Her brother is Freyr. Her husband was known as Odr. Many believe that he is Odin, Frigg's husband, and some even believe Frigg and Freya are in fact the same entity.

Freya has a fondness for material possessions, beauty, fertility, and love. Because of these interests, she is viewed as, what we would call in modern society, a party girl. Evidence can be found of this is in the poem where Loki accuses her of sleeping with every elf and God, even her brother.

She was a practitioner of seidr, an organized form of magic. She brought this skill to the gods and the humans. Since she was an expert at manipulating and controlling prosperity, health, and desires or other people, it would be safe to say that her power and knowledge are unmatchable.

Freya was a goddess of the afterlife, and ruled over a place in the afterlife called Folkvang. She chose half of all the slain warriors who died during battle to dwell there.

Freyr

Freyr, FREY-ur, meaning Lord, was a member of the Vanir and became an honorary god of Aesir after he was taken hostage during the war. He was one of the most idolized gods. It's not hard to understand why; their survival and well-being depended on him. This was manifested through peace, wealth, bountiful harvest, and ecological and sexual fertility. It should come as no surprise that he received sacrifices on many occasions.

If a sacrifice took place at a harvest festival, they would typically sacrifice a boar, his favored animal.

Njord was his father, and his mother is unnamed but is presumed to be Nerthus. Freyr has been a lover of several giantesses and goddesses, one of which is his sister, Freya. Incest was an acceptable and commonplace among the Vanir clan. This was not the case amongst historical Germanic people.

Freyr resided in Alfheim, which was the homeland of the elves. Many say that he ruled the elves, but there isn't any proof of this in Norse literature. The actual relationship between the gods and elves is scarce enough to cause several different assumptions.

One of his famous possessions was his ship, Skíðblaðnir. The ship always has the best wind and can be folded up so that it can fit into a small bag. Suggested by its name, the ship served as the archetype of ships that were built only for rituals and were never to be seaworthy. Freyr traveled on land in a chariot drawn by boars.

Njord

Njord is pronounced NYORD, the meaning of which is unknown. As with his children, he is not only a member of the Vanir but an honorary member of the Aesir. Nerthus is likely his sister as well as the mother of his children, Freya and Freyr.

He was associated with seafaring, the sea, fertility, and wealth. The Norse even had a saying for people who were wealthy. They would say "as rich as Njord."

He is most prominently featured in the story of Skadi. Skadi was a giantess and went to the Aesir for restitution of her father's murder. They told her that she could make any god her husband. She mistakenly picked Njord, thinking that he was Baldur. They had an unpleasant and short marriage. Part of their marriage was spent in her home in the snowy mountains; which Njord couldn't handle. The rest of the time was in Njord's home on the beach, which Skadi couldn't handle. They quickly parted ways.

Nerthus

Nerthus was an idolized goddess. She was known as Mother Earth. It was believed that she would take part in human activities and rode in a cow-drawn chariot among the humans. Only the priest was able to touch her, and join her in the chariot. He would follow her throughout the day and merrymake in every place that she wanted to visit. When she would visit an area, there would be no war, nobody would take up arms, and all iron would be locked away. It would stay like this until she returned to her home. When she returns, everything, even the goddess, would be cleansed in a lake. A slave would perform this cleanse before being drowned.

Historians can connect Nerthus to the Vanir based on her name. Nerthus, a Proto-Germanic name, would be spelled in Old Norse as Njord. There are two theories as to why this is. The first being that Njord and Nethurs are a divine pair. The other theory states that Nerthus and Njord were actually a hermaphroditic deity.

Gullveig

Gullveig, GULL-vayg, was a goddess that appeared in only two stanzas within the Voluspa. These verses describe everything that leads to the Aesir-Vanir War. From the verses, we learn that she was seidr, a practitioner of magic. It states that Gullveig had travelled to Aesir and performed magic that they viewed as dangerous and antisocial. They then tried to kill her. With magic, she was able to prevent her death.

Magic wasn't the only thing that she was able to mesmerize the Aesir with. Her name is a two part word. The first, gull, means gold, and the second, veig, means intoxication or alcoholic drink. This means that her name means nothing other than "the intoxication caused by a precious metal."

3 THE GREAT WAR

FOR THE MOST part, it can be difficult to tell which gods and goddesses belong to which clan, the Vanir or Aesir. There was one time in history where it was easy to tell the difference.

Freya, a Vanir goddess, traveled to Aesir using the name Heidr. She mesmerized the gods and goddesses with her power, and they sought after her service. They quickly realized that they had pushed aside their values of obedience, kin loyalty, and honor for their selfish desires. They started to blame Freya for their problems and named her Gullveig and tried to kill her. They tried burning her three times, and each time she was reborn.

Because of this experience, the two clans began hating and fearing each other. This caused a war to erupt. The Aesir used regular combat rules, and they fought with brute force and weapons. The Vanirs used magic. The war lasted for a long while, and each side had the upper hand at some point. Soon, both sides became tired of fighting and eventually called a truce. According to customs of the time, both sides paid tribute to each other, which consisted of sending a hostage to live in the other clan. The Vanir sent Njord, Freyr, and Freya, while the Aesir sent Mimir and Hoenir to Vanir.

Fortunately for Njord and his children, they lived somewhat peacefully in Asgard. The same cannot be said for Mimir and Hoenier. The Vanir quickly realized that Hoenir could give them fantastic advice for any problem, but they never realized that this was only true if he had Mimir with him. In truth, Hoenir was a slow-witted simpleton that never knew what to say unless he had Mimir with him. After Hoenir had given them the advice of "Let others decide" one time too many, they began to think that they had been cheated in the exchange. They decided to chop off Mimir's head and sent it back to Asgard. Odin quickly chanted some poems and embalmed it with herbs. He was able to preserve Mimi's head so that he was   able   to   receive   advice   in   times   of   need. They had no interest in restarting the war over this. Instead, they all came together and spat in a cauldron. Their saliva created Kvasir, who was the wisest of every being. This was a way for them to pledge and keep harmony to each other.

4 RAGNAROK

RAGNAROK MEANS "The Doom of the Gods." This is the name that the Norse gave to the ultimate end of their cosmos and then their re-creation. The word Ragnarok is a play on words, but we'll look at that a little later, first let's look at the story itself.

Dreams and prophecies had long existed and told the destruction of the cosmos and everything that lived in it. Once the first event came to pass, which was Baldur being killed Loki, the gods were forced to look at the fact that they couldn't escape their destiny. Odin began to gather the best human warriors to help him fight in his last battle against the giants. Even though they prepared, they knew that there was no way that they could stop their demise.

The human population abandoned their normal way of life and fell into a deep depression. The same could be said for the gods. Many broke oaths and fell short of many of their expectations. Three winters would come one right after another. There would be no summer between them. This devastating darkness and frigidity was prophesied as the Fimbulwinter, The Great Winter.

Loki and Fenrir broke free of their bindings and began wreaking havoc on the Nine Worlds. Yggdrasil, the great tree, soon began to tremble. Heimdall, the far-seeing, soon said that a massive army of giants was coming for the stronghold. Among them was Loki commanding Naglfar. Heimall alerted the gods.

The Giants began to destroy the world and the cosmos. Fenrir ran through the land, his upper jaw to the sky and his lower jaw on the land, and consumed everything between them. He even ate the sun. Surt, which was a giant with a sword of flame, ran across the world and left an inferno after him.

The gods fought courageously to their end. Thor and Jormungand killed one another, as well as Freyr and Surt, and Loki and Heimdall. Fenrir ate Tyr, and Odin and was subsequently killed by Vidar.

Finally, the land sank into the sea and disappeared under the waves. Ginnungagap, the anti-cosmos, reigned again. However, this didn't last forever. The earth was soon brought out of the ocean. Baldur came back from the underworld. The land was even more fruitful and lush than before. Lif and Lifthrasir, a human couple, awoke the world. The gods then returned and resumed their life.

Many people view Ragnarok as the same thing as the Christian "End of Times," but historians believe that it describes a cyclical end. This means that after destruction, there is a re-creation. This will then be followed by Ragnarok and so on, forever. So instead of a beginning and an end on a straight line, it is birth and death in a circle; a never ending cycle.

This is how people can come to understand the meaning of Ragnarok. You can see this sequence within everything, such as life between extinctions, the life of an organism, the moon phases, day and night, and the seasons. This means that the "Twilight of the Gods" shows what the pre-Christian Norse saw with each sunset, autumn, waning the moon, and the aging process of humans. This is how they sanctified their existence, and if they believed that if they lived their life according to this, they would live a holy life.

5 GIANTS

THE GIANTS ARE another spiritual being of the Norse belief. Their powers are equal to that of the two God clans. Their personality, though, is extremely different than the gods. The gods and giants are opposing forces.

The word giant is misleading. In today's time, giant draws to mind an enormously sized person. Instead, to the Norse, the word was used to describe a dreaded being in heathen times. Old Norse called them jotnar or pursar. The word jitunn means devourer. Pursar means the injurious one.

Why did the devourers become known as giants? When William the Conquerer took over England in 1066, French words started to make their way into the English language. Among these was the word geant, which soon became giant. Geant was the word they used to describe the fate in Greek mythology, which, like the giants in Norse mythology, were the enemies of the gods. Thus the devourers became known as the Giants.

Fenrir

Fenrir, FEN-reer, means the one who lives in the marshes. He is the most monstrous wolf in Norse mythology. He has been depicted on several runestones that have survived, and he is omnipresent in several literary sources. His father is Loki, and his mother is Angrboda, a giantess. Jormungand is his brother, and Hel is his sister.

Fenrir was viewed so fearfully by the other gods that they kept him in their stronghold. Tyr was the only one that was brave enough to feed him. As he grew, the gods tried to bind him. They tricked him into the chains by telling him it was to see how strong he was. They would cheer each time he would break free. They went to the dwarves to build a chain that couldn't be broken. They forged the chain from bird spittle, fish breath, mountain roots, a beard from a woman, and the footsteps of a cat. They called it Gleipnir, meaning open.

Fenrir was skeptical when presented with these chains, so he requested that a god or a goddess place their hand in his mouth as a sign of good faith. Tyr volunteered, and when Fenrir discovered he couldn't escape, he bit off Tyr's hand. They moved him to a desolate area and tied him to a boulder. They placed a sword in his mouth so that it would stay open. As he ceaselessly howled, a river, known as Expectation, flowed out of his lips. He remained there until Ragnarok.

Skadi

Skadi, SKAHD-ee, is a Norse mythology goddess and giantess. Her name may be related to the word skadi, meaning harm, or the word skadus, meaning shadow. Most likely her name is related to Scandinavia, but it remains unknown as for whether she lent her name to the land-mass or the other way around.

Her home is in the tallest part of the mountains where there is always snow. She is known for her hunting abilities, and you will never hear her mentioned without her skis, snowshoes, and bow.

The Giants are known for being a force of death and darkness, and this can easily be seen in Skadi's description. Since she did receive the status of a goddess when she married Njord, in addition to the traditional worship of her, means that she may have been more benevolent than her relatives.

Jormungand

Jormungand, YOUR-mun-gand, is a sea serpent, and his name means a great beast. He circles Midgard, which has given him the nickname of Midgard Serpent. He is so massive that his body encircles Midgard entirely.

He is the child of Angroboda and Loki, and his siblings are Fenrir and Hel. Thor is his biggest enemy. They fought on several occasions and ultimately killed each other during Ragnarok. Jormungand has been present in Germanic religions for a long time. An example of this is the fact that Germans blamed him for earthquakes.

Nidhogg

Nidhogg is one of the most famous serpents, and his name means curse-striker. He lives below Yggdrasil and feasts on its roots. This hurts the tree. He does this intentionally with a goal of pulling the world into chaos.

This would mean that he played an important part in Ragnarok. He is said to have flown out from Yggdrasil to help the giants in their battle.

In some ways, you could draw a parallel between Nidhogg and the

Biblical serpent in the Garden of Eden.

6 COSMOLOGY

THE NORSE BELIEF in the creation of the cosmos is an entertaining and colorful story that is full of meaning. Here is how the Norse believe the Nine Worlds were created:

Ginnungagap, a gaping abyss, existed before anything was created. This confusion of darkness and silence was located between Niflheim, the homeland of ice, and Muspelheim, the home of fire.

The flames coming from Muspelheim and the frost from Niflheim began to move towards each other. Through the sputter and hiss of the elements, the fire started to melt the ice. These drops quickly formed the first godlike giant, Ymir. This giant, a hermaphrodite, was able to reproduce asexually. Whenever he would sweat, Giants would be born.

Audhumbla, a cow, emerged from the melting frost next. Ymir was nourished from her milk, and salt-licks within the ice was able to nourish her. As she licked, she slowly found Buri, the first Aesir god. Buri then had a son, Bor, who would then marry Bestla, the daughter of Bolthorn, a giant. Bestal and Bor's half-giant and half-god children were Odin, Vili, and Ve.

Odin and his brothers set out to kill Ymir. They then began to construct their world with his corpse. The oceans were made of his blood, his muscles and skin formed the soil, his hair formed the vegetation, his brain made the clouds, and skull formed the sky. Four dwarves, the each corresponded with the four points, held the skull above everything.

The first man and woman were soon formed, Ask and Embla, from trunks from two trees. They then built a fence that protected their dwelling, Midgard, to help protect them from the giants.

The Nine Worlds

The Nine Worlds are where the beings of Old Norse and Germanic people lived. Their lands were within the roots and branches of the tree Yggdrasil. There is mention of their world in Poetic Edda, but there are few other sources that list exactly the worlds that made up the nine. By compiling some sources and at looking Norse mythology, we can come up with a possible list of the Nine Worlds:

Midgard – the human world
Asgard – the Aesir gods and goddesses world
Vanaheim – the Vanir gods and goddesses world
Jotunheim – the giant's world
Niflheim – the ice world
Muspelheim – the fire world
Alfheim – the elf world
Svartalfheim – the dwarf world
Hel – where the dead and goddess Hel resides

Except for Midgard, all the other worlds are pretty much invisible. Considering the pantheistic and animistic beliefs of the Norse, these worlds did manifest in some ways within the human world. You can see this in Jotunheim because it overlaps with the wilderness of the human world, Hel being the underworld that is beneath the earth, and Asgard as being the sky.

Nine also seems to hold some magical significance, but it hasn't be discovered quite yet. You can see the number nine pop up in several stories, such as the fact that Odin had hung from the tree for nine days and nights to discover the runes, Heimdall had nine mothers, and before he could marry Gerd, Freyr had to wait nine nights.

Yggdrasil

Yggdrasil, IG-druh-sill, is an ash tree that sits at the center of the cosmos. The tree grows from the Well of Urd. Yggdrasil holds, within its branches and roots, the Nine Worlds. The trees name probably looks pretty complicated to most modern people. Its translation means, "the ash tree of the horse of Yggr." The name Yggr was a nickname of Odin and means "The Terrible One." Even though it still seems to be a strange name for a tree, but you can better understand it if you look at the fact that it is used as transportation between the different worlds.

Then there's the Well of Urd. Urd, pronounced just as it's spelled, is translated to destiny. This means that you could call it the Well of Destiny.

Within the well lives three maidens known as the Norns, we will discuss more about them later.

Besides the Nine Worlds, other beings live around, on, in, and under the tree. Unfortunately, they are only mentioned in passing in most texts. Some of the most well known are the eagle that lives in the top branches, many dragons, and snakes, the most famous being Nidhogg, and Ratatosk, a squirrel. The squirrel would carry messages between the eagle and Nidhogg. There are also four deer, Dyrathror, Duneyr, Davalin, and Dain, which eat from the highest branches.

Midgard

Midgard, which means "Middle Enclosure," is the human world of the Nine Worlds. It somewhat corresponds with the modern English concept of the word civilization. Of the Nine Worlds, it is the only one that can be seen, even though the other worlds do intersect with different aspects of Midgard.

There is a double meaning to the word Midgard. The first is a literal meaning to the position of their world, which is in the middle of all the other worlds. It's surrounded by the Jotunheim wilderness; this much like how the continents of today are surrounded by the oceans. Midgard also has water that surrounds its world, and this is where Jormungand lives. Aegir and Ran also live in these waters and will take the life of unfortunate seafarers. This is somewhat of a horizontal meaning. The vertical meaning tells us its position between Asgard and the underworld. The axis here is represented by Yggdrasil, where Asgard is located at the top of the branches, Midgard at the trunk base, and the underworld in its roots.

Both of these senses of Midgard help to show us its literal, psychogeographical location in how the ancient Germanic people viewed their world. They believed in the land that was innangard, which means within a fence, was civilized, orderly, and law-abiding. They also saw land that was utangard, meaning past the wall, as wild and chaotic. This can be viewed within their geographical world and their psyche; your actions or thoughts have the capability to be utangard or innangard just as a location.

In their creation story, the gods used the corpse of Ymir to create their world, and they built a fence around Midgard using Ymir's eyebrows. This was done to protect them from the giants. This same practice could be seen in the real world of the time with farms. Farms would have fences around them to mark off that which is in and out.

Asgard

Asgard is the home of the Aesir gods and goddesses, and its literal meaning is "enclosure of the Aesir." Asgard is at the very top of the Yggdrasil and connects to Midgard with a rainbow bridge named Bifrost.

It was mentioned earlier about the beliefs of the ancient Germanic people of innangard and utangard, and the gard in the name Asgard is about those beliefs. Asgard is, of course, innangard. Asgard is partly surrounded by a wall built by Hrimthurs.

One of the most well-known places in Asgard is Valhalla, where Odin rules. Asgard is also a temple for 12 gods, Gladsheim, and their respective goddesses, Vingolf. The gods meet in Idavoll every day to discuss the fate of all the men and gods.

Vanaheim

Vanaheim means "homeland of the Vanir." Vanaheim is located around Yggdrasil, below Asgard. Most of the sources that have survived are fragmentary and don't explicitly mention the location of Vanaheim. The best clue is when the Poetic Edda says that Njord travels eastward to Asgard when he is sent as a hostage. That would mean that Vanaheim is likely west of Asgard.

It's no surprise that there is sparse information as to what kind of place Vanaheim is. Instead, we can draw some conclusions based on the name. If you go back to the ancient Germanic belief of innangard and utangard places, you will notice that Vanaheim doesn't end in gard. Only two worlds end in gard, Midgard, and Asgard. It would be safe to say that both Midgard and Asgard are surrounded by some fence. All the other worlds end in heim. This would mean that they aren't surrounded by a fence, and that would make them an utangard world. This would mean that the Vanir from Vanaheim is more natural than the Aesir who are more cultural.

Jotunheim

Jotunheim, YO-tun-hame, means the "world of the giants" and is home to the Giants in Old Norse belief. Utgard is another name for Jotunheim. It is also a combination of innangard and utangard. This shows that the realm holds a space at one extreme of their land beliefs. The wilderness comes from the Old English root words of wild-deor-ness, which translates to "the place of the self-willed beats." This means that Jotunheim is a wilderness which surrounds a civilized world.

The dwellings of the giants are known as mountain peaks within a dark, thick forest. It endlessly snows, and winter never eases up. Their landscapes are grim and inhospitable.

Ifing, a river, separates Asgard and Jotunheim. Jotunheim also held Gastropnir and Prymheim. King Thrym ruled the Giants. Gudmund lived in Glaesisvelli, another location in Jotunheim.

Niflheim

Niflheim, NIF-el-hame, is the "world of the fog" within the Nine Worlds. It is home to the ice, mist, cold, and darkness. It is the opposite of the world of Muspelheim. In their creation story, Ymir was formed by frost from Niflheim and the fire from Muspelheim.

There isn't much more on the Niflheim. In fact, it's only found in the words of Snorri Sturluson, an Icelandic historian. It is also used interchangeably with Niflehl, which was a description of the word Hel. Niflhel appears in works that are older than Snorri's, so it's quite possible that he made up the word Niflheim. Unfortunately, all the information surrounding these worlds comes from Snorri.

Muspelheim

Muspelheim, MOO-spell-hame, means "the world of Muspell." It is the home of the fire giants. Just like the world before, Muspelheim is only found in the works of Snorri Sturluson, which cannot be believed to authentically represent the pre-Christian Norse beliefs. The cosmological principles, though, can be traced back to ancient Germanic beliefs.

The word Muspell is found in Old Saxon and German texts, and holds the same concepts, which means it likely does date back to Old Norse. The oldest meaning of the word is likely "end of the world through fire." It refers to a giant, in Old Norse poetry, that led his people into the Ragnarok battle. Even if the world Muspelheim was a creation of Snorri's, it shouldn't be viewed as a problem considering the meaning of Muspell.

Muspelheim plays a part in the creation of the world, and the destruction of the world. When the world is created, fire and ice work together to form the first giant. In Ragnarok, Surt, a fire giant, comes with a flaming sword to kill the gods.

Aflheim

Alfheim, ALF-hame, means "the homeland of the elves." Just like the name tells you, this is where the elves live in Old Norse beliefs. There is very little description of Alfheim in source materials. It is only really mentioned in passing. The elves, though, are described. They are seen as being beautiful and luminous people. That would mean that their home would be full of light.

Freyr, a Vanir god, was the ruler of Alfheim. This has been a source of confusion as to why a god was a ruler over the elf world. There is a lot of overlap between the Vanir and the Elves, so it probably shouldn't be a surprise that Freyr is a Lord of Alfheim.

Svartalfheim / Nidavellir

The Dwarf world is referred to as Svartalfheim, SVART-alf-hame, or Nidavellir, NID-ud-vell-eer. They mean "homeland of the black elves" and "dark fields" respectively.

The Dwarves are known to be excellent craftsmen who live underground. This means that their world was likely an underground world of confusing forges and mines. Nidavellir was likely the original name of their home. Even though the use of both names occurs later in history and in sources that are problematic, Nidavellir appears for the first time in an older source than the only use of Scartalfheim.

Since the dwarves were master craftsmen, it's safe to assume that their world is going to be full of exquisite halls. Snorri, the only person to use the world Svartalfheim, causes more unnecessary confusion about the boundaries between the different worlds. He even confuses the dwarf Sindri as the name of the world itself.

This means that we still only have a vague idea of how the Vikings viewed the dwarf homeland.

Helheim

Helheim, most commonly shortened to Hel, is the name of the underworld. The goddess Hel oversees the world. Similar to Greek mythology, some sources say a dog guards its entrance.

The Norse world of Hel and the Christian belief of Hell are both similar in the fact they house the dead underground. Other than that, they have nothing else in common. Information on what happened after death in Old Norse belief isn't quite clear, but one thing is for sure: where a person went after they died wasn't based on how they lived their life.

When the underworld is described, it's generally cast in positive or neutral terms. It's an area where the dead would continue to live in some capacity. It's even portrayed as an area where life was abundant even after death. In Hel, the dead would spend their eating, sleeping, fighting, and drinking. It wasn't either eternal torment or bliss, but instead a continuation of life.

Snorri's Prose Edda is the only writing that ever portrays Hel as a negative place. As we have seen, he had a tendency to change things by stretching the information he had available. He wanted to make it seem as if his pre-Christian ancestors were anticipating the views of Christianity. There are very few scholars that accept Snorri's views of Hel.

7 DESTINY

ONE OF THE most extraordinary and key concepts of the pre-Christian Norse beliefs was their beliefs surrounding destiny, which was sometimes call urd in old Norse or wyrd in old English. The concept of Greek fate and the karma concept of Hinduism share the same Indo-European origin with Urd. But they are all still unique.

To begin understanding their views on destiny, you have to understand the significance of Yggdrasil and the Well of Urd. We've already covered these aspects, but as a reminder, Yggdrasil is a tree which holds the Nine Worlds that make up the cosmos. This tree grows from the Well of Urd. The image of water is a crucial part of their views on destiny

Their water cycle also gives further evidence on their world existing on a circular plane instead of a linear plane, as is thought of today. Their fate cycles through this and follows the course of the water. Destiny is the force which makes the past influence the present, which, then affects the past.

The Norns live inside the well and carve the destinies of the people and gods of the cosmos into the tree. This gives us another image of the past, which is the well, influencing the present, which is the tree. Everybody that lives within the cosmos is subject to the carvings of the Norns.

However, this is an imperative thing to understand, what the Norns carve is only the earliest possible outcome that a person can have, not the only outcome. Unlike Greek Fates, the Norns word isn't necessarily absolute.

Everybody that is subject to destiny has the power to change their destiny, as well as other people's destinies. This power is used passively by everyone, in one way or another.

There are some, though, that will take this process in their hands and actively change the destiny of people. They use magic to change destinies. There may only be three main Norns, capital "N," there are several other norns, lowercase "n," that are magic practitioners. The Norns may be able to shape somebody's destiny, but they are far from the only people that can alter futures course.

8 VALKYRIES

THE VALKYRIE, VAL-ker-ee, are female spirits that help Odin. Their name means the "choosers of the fallen." In the modern world, Valkyries are seen as noble and elegant maidens that carry dead heroes to Valhalla. This is a relatively accurate view, but it's selective and seems to exaggerate their nicer qualities. Some sources like to sanitize the Valkyrie, choosing to focus on them assisting Odin in brings his favorite slain warriors to Valhalla, and their affairs with men.

According to history, these characteristics are all true, but during heathen times they were likely also more mischievous. Not only do they get to pick the slain that are allowed to live in Valhalla and fight with Odin during Ragnarok, but they also get to pick the people that are slain during a battle. They can use magic to make sure that their deaths do happen. There are many examples of the Valkyries hand picking the people that get to live or die. One of the most gruesome stories is where twelve valkyries, before the Battle of Clontarf, sit and weave the destiny to the battle. The thread is made from intestines; they use heads for weights, and arrows and swords for needles. As they weave they chant in haunting joy.

9 VALHALLA

VALHALLA MEANS THE hall of the fallen and is where Odin allows the dead he deems worthy to live. Valhalla is described as gold and bright. The roof is made of shields, and its rafters are made of spears. The feasting tables are surrounded with seats made out of breastplates. Wolves guard the gates, and an eagle soars above.

Snorri Sturluson is the only person that has written about how a person got to join Valhalla. He stretched the truth on a lot of things, so he's not necessarily a reliable source. He stated that anybody that died during battle got to enter Valhalla. He also said that anybody who died of natural causes or sickness would go to Hel.

He then contradicts this when he talks about the death of Baldur. There are no other sources that state these reasonings. Many other sources contradict Snorri's beliefs as well. It's very likely that Snorri fabricated these small distinctions between Valhalla and Hel based on his Christian beliefs.

Even still, he probably wasn't completely wrong. Entrance into Valhalla was mainly whoever the Valkyries and Odin chose, and it would probably be safe to say that they would pick warriors because they were ultimately going to be a part of Odin's army.

Some descriptions of Valhalla have the great hall being located in Asgard, but some sources suggest that it may have been located underground. The constant battle that takes place is Valhalla's defining feature.

10 EINHERJAR

EINHERJAR, ane-HAIR-yar, is the name given to the spirits of dead warriors that live in Valhalla. The word einherjar means "those who fight alone." Viking warriors dreamed of becoming Einherjar when they died.

The Einherjar are the dead that resides inside. These warriors are the envy of Viking warriors. During the day they fight each other and perform other courageous deeds. Each night their wounds heal, and they receive full health. Their dinners are huge to help refuel them after a day full of battles. They eat meat from Saehrimnir, a boar that is brought back to life each time he is butchered. The goat Heidrun gives them mead to drink. This means that they get to enjoy an endless supply of delicious food and beverages. The Valkyries wait on them.

Odin didn't keep einherjar just for the ostentatious amusement. He had a purpose, and all the einherjar were handpicked with this purpose in mind. The Einherjar is meant to fight beside Odin during his final battle during Ragnarok. Despite their effort, they will all fall when Odin does, and fall away with the cosmos.

The definition of their name is confusing because there isn't any material that states that they ever fight alone. Some have surmised that the word may have come from an older root that meant "those who belong to an army." This definition may make more sense than the previous suggestion.

11 THE NORNS

THE NORNS ARE three females that control the destiny of the cosmos; more so than anybody else in the universe. They live in the Well of Urd which is located underneath Yggdrasil. They have control over destiny by carving runes into the tree's trunk. In some stories, they weave destiny in a tapestry or a web.

The etymology of the word is uncertain. It's believed that it may come from a word meaning "to twine." Some believe that it may be related to the Swedish dialect word norna, which means to "secretly communicate."

The names of the women are Skuld, "what shall be," Verdandi, "what is coming into being," and Urd, "what once was." A big misconception some people have about the women is that they correspond to the linear concept of the past, present, and future. A better way to look at is, is they are the past, present, and necessity. These work better in the cyclical concept of their world. It's even easier to view them as each representing a part of destiny that are intertwined and flow along with time.

Each morning the Norns begin by setting a rooster on top of Yggdrasil. The rooster is used to wake up all the gods and goddesses of Asgard. After that, they take water from the Well of Urd, and water Yggdrasil with it. This is an important part of keeping the tree healthy and green. The people of the Viking Age respected the Norns. It was common practice to serve somebody that had just given birth a bowl of porridge, which was known as Norn porridge. The Vikings also thought that the Norns were close whenever there was a birth. The porridge was an offering. They hoped to please the Norns so that they would make sure the child and mother had good health.

The Norns were seen as giantesses. When they came to the tree from Jotunheim, they brought an end the god's golden age. In stories when the Norns make an appearance, when the Norns pass judgment, it would mean death for the person, or persons, that were judged.

Snorri writes about other, lesser-known, Norns. He claims that there are different races of Norns. Basically, he believed that there were Norns from each inhabited world. As we've discussed earlier, some of Snorri's writing can't be fully accepted. He enjoyed stretching the truth.

When a new child was born, the Norns would visit the child to decide what its future would hold. Everybody's fate within the cosmos depends on how malevolent and benevolent the Norns were being. Whenever somebody constantly had bad things happening to them, they would blame the Norns for their problems. It's also believed that Skuld, the youngest Norn, is a Valkyrie as well.

12 KVASIR

KVASIR, KVAHSS-eer, was created by the Vanir and Aesir god at the end of their war. The ended the war with a truce. They sealed their truce by creating an alcoholic drink together, through a communal and ancient method. This process involved all of them chewing berries and spitting them into a cauldron. They then fermented the liquid. This liquid turned until the god Kvasir. His name likely came from the Norwegian word kvase, which means, "fermented berry juice."

He was the wisest of all the beings in the cosmos. He always had an answer to every question that was asked of him. He became a wanderer and traveled around sharing his wisdom with everybody he met along the way. He came to the house of Galar and Fjalar, two dwarves; they ended up killing him and drained him of all his blood. They placed his blood in three containers. They lied to the gods and said he suffocated from having too much wisdom. They then created mead by mixing honey with his blood, thus creating the Mead of Poetry.

There isn't any evidence that there was ever a more than one Kvasir. In everything about him, he was a sole figure who exemplified the qualities of the mead of poetry. After its creation, the mead quickly became the property of Odin. This is why many of Kvasir's characteristics are also associated with Odin.

13 THE MEAD OF POETRY

A S STATED ABOVE, Kvasir was created from the spit of the gods and was the wisest of all beings. He encountered his demise at the hands of two dwarves, who then brewed him into the mead of poetry. The mead held Kvasir's wisdom and was named Odroerir, "stirrer of inspiration," and anybody that drank the mead would become a scholar or poet.

The dwarves apparently enjoyed murder. Not long after, they took Gilling, a giant, out to sea to drown him for the fun of it. The noise that Gilling's wife made when crying bothered the dwarves, so they killed her too. They killed her by dropping a millstone on her as she walked into their home.

This last stunt got them into trouble. Once Suttung, Gilling's son, found out about his father's death, he took the dwarves out to a reef during low tide. The dwarves began to beg to be released, and Suttung agreed only if they would give him all of the mead that they had made from Kavasir. He then hid all of the mead in a hidden chamber within the Hnitbjorg Mountain. He had his daughter, Gunnlod, protect the mead.

Odin, who was always looking expand his wisdom, was unhappy with the fact the mead was being hoarded away. He quickly set out to acquire the mead for himself, and for any person that he felt was worthy.

He disguised himself as a farmhand and traveled to Baugi's, Suttung's brother, farm. When he arrived, nine servants were mowing the hay. As he approached them, he took a whetstone out of his cloak and asked if they wanted him to sharpen their scythes. They all agreed, and after he had finished, they were amazed at how well they worked. They all marveled over the whetstone, and they all wanted to purchase it. Odin said he would sell it, but he told them that it would come at a price. He threw the stone in the air. All the servants began to scramble to catch it, and they ended up killing each other.

Odin made his way to Baugi's house and told him he was Bolverkr. He told him that he could do all the work of the servants, who, he lied, had killed each other because of a dispute. He told Baugi that in return he wanted a sip of the mead.

Baugi told him that he didn't control Suttung's mead, but if he could perform all of the work that the nine men had to do, that he would help him try to get some of the mead.

Once the growing season had ended, Odin had held up his end of the deal. Baugi agreed to go with him to Suttung's to ask him about his mead. Suttung quickly and angrily refused. Odin, still in disguise, reminded Baugi of their deal. He convinced Baugi to help him get into the Gunnlod's dwelling. They traveled to an area of the mountain that Baugi believed to closest to the chamber. Odin pulled out an auger and gave it to Baugi so he could drill into the rock. The giant did as he was told and began drilling. He quickly told Odin he was finished. Odin blew in the hole, and the dust blew in his face. Odin told Baugi that he needed to finish drilling through the rock. Baugi once again began to drill and then told Odin he was finished. This time, when Odin blew in the whole, the debris went through.

Odin thanked him and then turned into a snake. He slithered into the hole, and Baugi tried to stab him, but he was able to wiggle away.

Once he made it inside, he changed into a charming man and walked over to Gunnlod. He quickly tricked her into trusting him and promised to allow him three sips of mead if he slept with her for three nights. On the third night, Odin consumed the contents of each container in one sip.

He quickly switched into an eagle and flew back to Asgard. Suttung quickly discovered what had happened and transformed into an eagle as well, and took off after him.

When the other Aesir gods saw Odin being followed by Suttung, they sent several vessels out to protect him. Odin made it into Asgard before Suttung could catch up. Suttung angrily retreated. Odin regurgitated all of the mead into his containers. During this, some drops fell off of his beak and landed in Midgard. These drops are where mediocre, and bad scholars and poets come from. The real scholars and poets are handpicked by Odin and given some of the mead with care.

Even though this tale is entertaining, it also shows big differences in how we view the world today and how pre-Christian Germanic people saw the world.

Today, we believe that we have control of how own thoughts and beliefs. This is what we call reason. To begin our reasoning process we have to make an assumption, which is something that a person doesn't have proof of but can accept based on its merits. We do this because of infinite regress. This means that each statement a person tries to prove, a new statement has to be added to continue to support the original statement, and this continues indefinitely until somebody comes to an indivisible truth. When and why is this stopped? When do we know that we have found something that is so perfectly sound that it would be idiotic to try to question its truth?

The story of the Mead of Poetry shows us that pre-Christian people believed that they received insights and knowledge from Odin instead of logical proof.

Using mead isn't a random choice either. One of their main rituals, sumbl, centered around drinking alcohol to enter a state of ecstasy. They believed that people were able to understand the truth in this kind of state. In this context, the person who is drinking becomes closer to the gods.

14 DISIR

THE DISIR, DEE-seer, are female spirits. It is nearly impossible to be able to distinguish between the Disir and the other spiritual beings clearly. An example of this are the Valkyries, which are female spirits that help Odin, and are sometimes called "Odin's Disir." The Disir are also described as being both benevolent and malevolent, just like the Valkyrie.

The Disir played a part in the fate of every person, as well as their attributes and wellbeing like luck, and represent death is some instances.
They are most often portrayed as being a guardian of a certain location, person, or group. When portrayed as such, they are never distinguished from other guardians like the hamingjur, gylgjur, and land spirits.

The Disir are typically depicted as being the spirit of a deceased female ancestor whose job to look after their descendants. This also shows some degree of overlap with them and the elves, which are typically depicted the same way.

Sometime during the winter, times varied across the lands, they would hold a festival to honor the Disir. In Iceland and Norway, they called the festival disablot, and it was held at the start of winter. They would keep it in either a temple of a house. It depended on if they could find an available temple. Judging by its name, they probably made a sacrifice as part of the ritual, and the sacrifice was followed by a lavish banquet. During their festival, they often celebrated the Valkyrie at the same time.Sweden held their festival, Disting, at the start of February, but there is even less information on their festival.

In some Old Norse literature, they used the word dis, which is the singular of disir and means goddess or woman. So how can we know who the Disir are?

It has to be remembered that the pre-Christian society was not codified or systematized. They never had a set of doctrines as to what dis meant, or for any word. It's easy to see why there is a lot of contradiction and confusion in the different texts. This particular religion was considered a living tradition and went through several changes during its time, just like every living tradition.

Depending on what text you read, you will get a different answer as to who the Disir are. It also depends on which person, place, group, and time you ask. The only commonality they all had was the fact that they were female. They seem to be a distinct spiritual group, at least different enough for them to have a festival about, but still impossible to clearly distinguish them from other female spiritual beings. Everything else is up to your personal interpretation.

15 THE WILD HUNT

THE WILD HUNT is a common tale in several ancient stories. Scandinavia called the wild hunt Oskoreia, which means "terrifying ride," or odensjakt, which means "Odin's hunt." It would move through the forest during the midwinter, which is the darkest and coldest time during the year. If someone found themselves outside after dark, they may be able to see this ghostly procession. If they were unlucky, the wild hunt may spot them, which would mean that they could be carried miles away from their home, or worse. Some magic practitioners allowed themselves to be taken, but while their body laid in their bed as if they were asleep. The wild hunt would wreck havoc in a town.

There are many stories about the wild hunt, all of which mention different leaders. However, even though there are several versions, there is one figure that was closely related to the wild hunt: Odin. Two of the nicknames given to Odin show that he is associated with midwinter as well, which was when the holiday Yule fell. Myths said that he would ride through the Nine Worlds on his horse Sleipnir, on a shamanic quest, which also connects him in another way to the wild hunt.

16 ASK AND EMBLA

ASK, ALSO SPELLED as Askr in Old Norse meaning "ash tree," and Embla, meaning "water pot" were the first humans of Midgard. Once the Aesir gods finished building the cosmos, they made Ask and Embla from tree trunks that had come upon the shore of the land that the gods had just pulled from the waters. Led by Odin, the gods gave these newly created humans the ability of ond, "breath or spirit," la, and odr, "ecstasy or inspiration." Nobody knows precisely what la means. Midgard was given to Ask and Embla, for them to live on, which made them the mother and father of the human race.

The story of Ask and Embla is full of meaning.

The fact that they name their first man "ash tree" and their first woman "water pot," they connect the first couple with the tree and the well. By doing this, they show that femininity and masculinity are complementary, reciprocal, and intertwined principles. This makes each aspect just as important as the other to ensure that life continues. This same male and female connection can be seen in Adam and Eve of the monotheistic religions that dominate the world today.

There are many different versions of the pre-Christian mythology. Many of these tell us what first appear to be accounts of contradictory human origins. In some, they say that people come from gods. In others, they say human tribes are descended from tree groves.

When you look at these stories and little more carefully, you will find that they are telling the same creation story of Ask and Embla, which tell both of the above ideas. It teaches us that humans come from trees, weather washed up on the beach or a grove and telling us that the gods created them. Pre-Chrisitan views see gods and goddesses as invisible forces that animate things in the visible world, unlike the views of God in a monotheistic religion. Since, in the creation story, everything is formed from the corpse of Ymir, all life comes from this one figure.

17 SLEIPNIR

SLEIPNIR, SLAYP-neer, is Odin's eight-legged horse. He one of the several shamanic spirits that Odin owns, other include Hugin and Munin, and the Valkyries. Sleipnir is probably able to be classified as a fylgja, which means an accompanying spirit. Odin rides him throughout the Nine Worlds when he goes on his adventures.

Having an eight-legged horse is a common motif for shamans. The use of them can be seen in many indigenous traditions throughout the world. Sleipnir was born from Loki after he turned himself into a mare and courted the stallion of a giant. This story is found in the Fortification of Asgard:

A Smith came to Asgard one day and offered to build a wall around their home to help protect them from anything that meant to do them any harm. The Smith was likely a giant, and he said he was able to do the work in just three seasons, but he demanded that he get to marry Freya, and the moon and the sun.

The gods spoke with each other. Freya was against the idea from the get go. Loki then suggested that they should give the builder want he wanted, but only if he can complete the build in a single winter with only the help of his horse. After awhile, the gods agreed to Loki's plan. Of course, they never planned on giving the builder the moon, sun, or Freya. They assumed that the task would be too hard to achieve.

The builder agreed to their new terms, only if the gods would swear oaths to make sure that the kept their promise, and that he would remain safe while in Asgard.

The Smith began to build the wall, and the gods were amazed at how fast he was able to build it. What they found even more confusing was the fact that the stallion, Svadilfari, was doing twice as much work as the builder. The stallion was able to haul huge boulders across long distances to add to the construction. When it approached the end of the winter, he had already built the wall so high that it was almost impenetrable by any enemy, and, alarmingly, wouldn't take too much longer to finish. The stones around the gate were the only thing that hadn't been placed.

The gods fussed at Loki for having given them such bad advice. They threatened to kill him if he didn't figure out how to prevent the builder from finishing the wall on time. Loki begged them not to kill him and swore his oath that he would do as the gods wish.

When night fell, the builder and his horse ventured into the forest looking for stones. Loki, in disguise as a mare, met them along their way. He whinnied at the stallion. Once the stallion spotted the mare, his heart was the only part of him that was excited by the horse. He broke his reigns and took after her. The horses ran all night long. The next morning the giant still couldn't find his horse, and giant now knew that he wouldn't be able to finish the wall on time.

The gods then gave the giant the payment they thought he deserved: a fatal hit from Thor's hammer that shattered his head into breadcrumb sized pieces.

Meanwhile, in the forest, the giant's stallion had caught up to Loki in mare form. Soon after, Loki gave birth to Sleipnir, the horse that would become Odin's steed.

18 ASATRU

ASATRU IS THE modern religion based on the pre-Christian Germanic views. Asatru builds on the surviving records of their past belief system, and the followers have worked hard to keep as close as possible to the religion of the original Norse people.

Asatru loosely means "belief in the sir," which likely means the gods. Broken down, Asatra is made of "asa" is the possessive of 'sir, meaning Aesir, and "tru" which is religion or belief.

In 1972 Asatru became recognized as a legitimate religion thanks to the poet Godi Sveinbjorn Beinteinsson. Since then, the religion has started to rapidly grow among former Norse countries, as well as in North America and Europe.

It's common for many religions to become corrupted with homophobic, sexist, racist, and anti-semitic beliefs. Fortunately for Asatru, since its resurgence, it has not been subject to any such corruption. In fact, they are strongly against racism and many other corruptions. Many groups even have these rules written into their constitutions. This applies to most English-speaking countries as well. Although there have been some anti-racism groups that have mistakenly called Asatru, as a religion, racist.

Here's how the Asatru belief system works:

They are polytheistic. They believe that there are three main races of Deities that live among, and are involved in the human life. These are the Aesir, Vanir, and Jotnar. They also worship the same gods and goddesses that we have already talked about. The most common are Thor, Odin, Freyr, Freya, Frigg, Skadi, and Ostara. They also honor the land spirits known as Landvaettir.

The North American Asatruars have come up with a list of the Nine

Noble Virtues: perseverance, self-reliance, industriousness, hospitality, discipline, fidelity, honor, truth, and courage. They place great importance on the family. They also reject all forms of discrimination based on sexual orientation, race, nationality, language, gender, or ethnicity, as well as any "other divisive criteria."

Their origin story follows the same origin story that the Old Norse people believed. Everybody is descended from Gods and Odin, Vili, and Ve made the first people Ask and Embla. Rig, another deity, came along and created the different social classes.

They believe in a gift of ecstasy, called od, given to them by the Gods. This is what they consider to separate the humans from the other animals, and is the eternal link to all the Gods.

Unlike the mainstream religions that believe a person goes to heaven or hell once they die based on how they lived their life, the Asatruar believe there are several afterlife locations. The heroic individuals and warriors go to Folkvangr, Freyja's field. This is where everybody wants to go. Then you have Helheim, which is the neutral realm that most people end up. Dishonorable people or oath breakers are consumed by Niddhog. Then the ones that die at sea are said to go to a different afterlife. However, many followers don't actually take the Norse myths literally. Many believe that they will be reincarnated along their family line. Then there are others that believe that the dead only inhabits their graves.

Of course, they believe that the end of the world will be Ragnarok, as explained above. At the end of the great battle, one man and woman will remain to repopulate the world and to live the same cycle over again

19 RUNES

THE ANCIENT GERMANIC system for writing used a runic alphabet. The runes worked similar to letters, but they are very different from how we view letters today. Each one was analogous to a pictographic symbol that represented some principle. When one wrote a rune, they invoked the power for which the image stood. The runes each had a name that hinted to a magical significance. They called their alphabets "futharks" which corresponds to the first six runes. Traditionally, runes would be carved into metal, bone, wood, stone, or other hard surfaces.

Their Origins

There are many arguments about the details of runic writing, but there is a general agreement in its outline. The runes are believed to have come from some of the Old Italic alphabets that were used among Mediterranean people during the first century. Other early Germanic symbols were influential in the runic script development as well.

The earliest runic inscription can be found on a brooch that was made in an area north of what is now Germany, in 50 CE. The inscription is debated, and many are divided about whether the inscription is Roman or runic. The earliest inscriptions that aren't disputed were found on a comb from Vimose and on a spearhead that came from Norway. Both date to around 160 CE. The earliest carving of the whole futhark is on the Kylver stone located Gotland, Sweden. This dates to around 400 CE.

Even though scholars have tried to discover where the runic alphabet was derived from, the ancient Germanic people never believed that the runes ever came from a mundane source such as the Old Italic alphabet. They didn't see the runes as something that was invented. They have always been and pre-existed Odin himself until he was able to discover them.

The runes of the Old Norse mythology were carved on the tree Yggdrasil by the Norns. This helps to prove the belief that when somebody wrote a rune, they released the power of what was being written.

It could be presumed that after Odin discovers the runes that he then was the one who gave the knowledge of the runes to the first human runemaster.

Philosophy and Magic

In the Old Norse world, spoken word had strong powers. They believed that anything that was spoken had great power and influence in their life. Once something was said, whatever happened afterward couldn't be changed, and they could never take back what was said. They believed that words made the reality, and not that reality made words. It's not that words reflect a person's perception of the world, but, instead, a person's experience and understanding of the world is affected by the things their language demands. Saying what you think was unheard of because they believed once it was said; it would change the course of reality.

Each rune was a representation of a phoneme, which is the smallest unit of sound, making it a visual form of a phoneme.

Many linguists don't look at the relationships between the meaning of a word and the sound of the word. Some scholars embrace this belief, which is called phonosemantics. This means that there is a connection between the sound a word makes and its meaning. Another way to look at this is that fact that each phoneme had its meaning. For example, look at the work thorn. It is built by the phonemes "th", "o", "r", and "n".

Phonosemantic view ties back into the belief that words can create a reality and not reality forming words. Since runes are a drawing of phonemes, that causes them to bring about the creative power of language into a visual medium. Rune's second meaning is a letter; its first is secret. This can be seen in the story where Odin discovered the Runes. If they weren't a secret, he wouldn't have had to go through what he did to discover them.

The runes were able to be used by both non-humans and humankind. This gave the two a way to communicate with each other and provided them with the basis of many magical acts.

20 THE SELF AND ITS PARTS

IN TODAY'S WORLD, most people look at their self as being comprised of three a particular, the mind, body, and soul. These parts form a whole that is clearly separated from the environment. These lines are pretty much absolute and cannot be changed.

In the Norse view, self is a tad more complicated. They may have had a view of the self; but they didn't have a "oneness" that they perceived. The self they believed in was made up of several parts that are all somewhat autonomous and can detach under the right circumstances. None of which correspond with a soul.

There are four important parts that help to make up the self; these include the hamr, hugr, fylgja, and the hamingja.

The Hamr

The meaning of hamr means to "skin" or "shape." This is a person's appearance, what other people perceive a person to look like based on observation. Unlike how we see things today, this perception isn't unalterable and absolute. Hamr is one of the most important words in their lexicon surrounding shapeshifting. The phrase they used for shapeshifting was "skipta homum" which translates to "changing hamr." The ability to do this was referred to as "hamramr" or "of strong hamr".

The Hamingja

The next part we will look at is the hamingja, pronounced HAHM-ing-ya. This is used to signify luck abstractly, but the way the Norse understood luck, is very different than how we look at luck. Luck is an entity of its own.

It is part of a person and can split from the self under certain circumstances. After a person passes away, their hamingja is reincarnated into a descendant, especially if a child is given their name. There are sometimes that the hamingya will bequeaths itself to a relative on its own. It can also be lent to a person when they are facing problems.

The Fylgja

The fylgja, FLIG-yur, are familiar spirits that follow people. This is most commonly seen in European folktales. Typically they are only seen by people blessed with second sight, but a human fylgjur isn't completely unheard of. They are a spirit whose well-being is linked to their owners.

This means if a fylgja were to die, then so would its own, and vice-versa. A person's fylgja normally comes in a form that is associated with their character. A noble person would likely have a bear, a violent person would have the wolf, and a pig would be given to a gluttonous person.

The Hugr

The last part we will look at is the Hugr. Hugr is best translated to mean "mind" or "thought." This part corresponds to a person's cognitive processes and is what we would see as an inner self. This part normally stays inside its owner, but can sometimes cause something to happen to a person just by thinking about them. This is prevalent in people that have an unyielding hugr.

21 DEATH AND THE AFTERLIFE

THERE WERE NEVER any actual Norse doctrines containing what happened to people after they died. Even though there aren't any certain views on life after death, there are some sources that perceive their afterlife as something other than chaos. There are some discernible patterns as to how the Norse people saw death and afterlife.

The spiritual parts of the deceased were thought to go to a certain otherworld. The most famous one would be that of Valhalla. The people that were personally chosen by Odin and his Valkyries got to spend their eternity in Valhalla preparing for Ragnarok.

Another hall is Folkvang that is ruled by Freya. Sadly, Folkvang, meaning "the field of the people" is only mentioned sparsely in some texts. This means that we don't know what kind of place it was like.

Anybody that died at sea, which was a relatively common occurrence given the seafaring culture of the time, are sometimes said to be taken to the underwater abode of Ran, a giantess.

The most common world that people went when they died was Hel, which is the underworld that was looked over by the goddess Hel. Besides being the general underworld, they also tell us that families would remain together in one area close to the area that they had lived when living.

The life in the afterlife was much like that of their living life. They practiced magic, slept, fought, caroused, drank, and ate. The differentiation of the different afterlives is blurry, and there isn't one definitive understanding as to how a person gets sent to a specific world.

There are also some sources that talk about people who die as being reborn as one of their descendants. They are never reborn into a different bloodline. Most of the time, they would be born as somebody in their lineage that was given their name.

Most people today look at the afterlife as being a reward or punishment for how they have lived their life. The Norse people didn't hold these types of views. Salvation and damnation were never a part of their worldview. So anybody that goes looking for a place similar to Heaven or Hell amongst the afterlife dwellings in Norse belief isn't going to find anything. The words Hell and Hel do come from the same root word, but the location and name are the only things the two have in common.

There is one text that makes mention of an afterlife that does punish people when they die: Nastrond, which means "shore of corpses." It contains a north-facing gate, a ceiling which drips poison, and a snake coils along the floor. The problem is that the poem is heavily influenced by Christianity.

CONCLUSION

Thank for making it through to the end of Norse Mythology. I hope it was informative and able to provide you with the information that you were looking for.

I hope you enjoyed learning about the vast information that surrounds the Old Norse belief system, even if some the history is sparse and incomplete.

Finally, if you found this book useful in any way, a review on Amazon is always appreciated!

ABOUT THE AUTHOR

Dustin Yarc is an ambitious Canadian author who writes passionately about his hobbies and areas of expertise such as personal development, spirituality, video games, gardening, and cryptocurrencies. He self-published his first title at the age of eighteen.